BOTTOM DOG PRESS
HURON, OHIO

INQUIRIES

POEMS

Jeff Gundy

**Photos by
Gregg Luginbuhl**

**Ohio Writers Series
Bottom Dog Press
Huron, Ohio**

Credits

My thanks to the editors of the periodicals and anthologies in which these poems originally appeared, some in different versions:

Artful Dodge: "Inquiry on the Fire Sermon," "Inquiry into Lagniappe"; *Beloit Poetry Journal*: "Inquiries into the Technology of Hell and Certain Rumors Recently Circulating," "In Response to Inquiries on the Dialectics of Consumption," "Inquiry into the Discovery of the City into Which the Saints Have Been Said to Go, Marching"; *Cincinnati Poetry Review*: "Inquiry into Simply Responding in the Negative," "Inquiry on Infections," "Inquiry into the Existential Maneuvers of Avians, or Honkers," "Inquiry into Keeping Time"; *Cornfield Review*: "Inquiry on the Son of a Practical Man" (as "Sketch of the Son of a Practical Man"); *Flights*: "Inquiry into What One Can Do with a Rented Jackhammer"; *From the Heartlands* (Bottom Dog, 1988): "Inquiry into the `Nearest of the Energies of the Universe and the Greatest Within the Range of Man's Needs'"; *The Gamut*: "Chainsaw Inquiries"; *The Journal*: "Inquiry on the Analogical Perspective, Or Why on This Day The Poet Will Enter No Complaints," "Inquiry into Lightness"; *The Laurel Review*: "Inquiry into the Nurturing and Elimination of Life Forms Within Marginally Controlled Ecosystems on the Fifteenth Anniversary of My Wedding"; *Mid-American Review*: "Inquiry into Praises" *Millstream Valley Express*: "Inquiry into Good Rains in August, or the Weeds"; *Ohio Review*: "Inquiry into the Origins of Hatred," "Inquiry into the Technology of Beauty"; *Pikestaff Forum*: "Inquiry into Faces, Light, the Guilt of Metaphor"; *The Rolling Coulter*: "Further Inquiries into the Nearest of the Energies of the Universe," "Inquiry on the Proposition that All Things Work Together for the Glory of the Father"; *Spoon River Quarterly*: "Inquiry into the Nature of Beauty, or the Tale of the King of the Cats," "Inquiry into Gifts, or the Indigo Bunting."

I also wish to thank the **Ohio Arts Council** for support during the preparation of this manuscript.
For advice, counsel and friendship I am grateful to Roger Mitchell, Lee Bahan, Dean Young, Keith Ratzlaff, Kevin Stein, Scott Sanders, Andrew Hudgins, and my first and best teacher, Nicholas Lindsay.

Contents

I.

II.

III.

IV.

in quire [ME. enqueren < OFr. **enquerre** < VL. *inquarere, for L. **inquirere** < **in,** into + **quaerere**, to seek] 1. to seek information; ask a question or questions 2. to carry out an examination or investigation . . .
in quir y n., pl. **-quir ies** 1. the act of inquiring

Webster's New World Dictionary

Seek and learn to recognize who and what,
in the midst of the inferno, are not the inferno,
then make them endure, give them space.

Italo Calvino, *Invisible Cities*

Marlyce, Nathan,
Ben and Joel—
This book is for you.

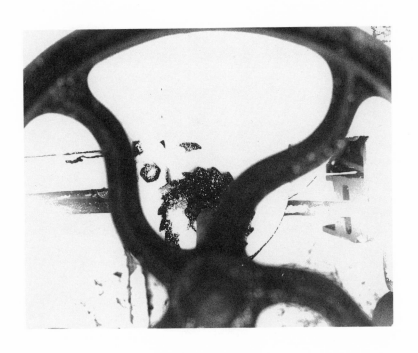

I

Inquiry into the "Nearest of the Energies of the Universe and the Greatest Within the Range of Man's Needs"

> "Wind and water are also primitive approaches to natural energies, but these change nothing while fire is a transforming agent."
> -Walter Hough, *Fire as an Agent in Human Culture*

> "And the men?
> They voted against
> themselves again
> and for fire . . .
> fire
> which voted for blackened stumps
> and no more elections."
> -Leonard Nathan, "The Election"

1.

It's the great fact of modern time, though mostly it happens out of sight. Remember visiting the coal-fired plants in junior high, riding on the school bus, sharing sack lunches, being led around through gray noisy forests of metal by a testy man in a hardhat? The great conveyors, the mountains of coal, the statistics, you and your friends oohing predictably in between, trying to make wisecracks that would impress the cutest girls? Did they let you see into the firechambers? Did they talk about wind patterns and particulate matter? Did it occur to you that some things had not been discussed? Not to me.

2.

In the summer of '73 a guy I worked with at the sash and door factory somehow decided I had agreed to go with him to see the nuke plant at Benton Harbor one Sunday. He woke me up banging on the door of the dark apartment in the converted church where I lived and it took me fifteen minutes to convince him that I hadn't said I would go and didn't intend to. They have a nice picnic area, he said, it'll be a nice drive. I went back to bed.

3.

Uncle Vernon splashed something on the charcoal and struck a match. Get back, he said, then when I barely moved, Get *Back*! He let the match drop and the gasoline burst outward like a hot flower living at ten times our speed. Oh, I said.

4.

The use of smoke in worship, I learn, "seems to have arisen from the observation that this ghostly element of combustion dissolved in the air, thus supplying a messenger to the unseen." The message turns out to be more practical and direct than we thought; God may be sniffing and noticing out there somewhere, but the agitated molecules bouncing back into the biosphere, shifting the jet stream and the Pacific currents, are what cut the cake.

5.

The green letters appear on the screen like elementals summoned from the void, obedient only because I know their names. I shuffle and demand them, bored, using them like wrenches and screwdrivers. If I could track them back through the chips and processors, wires and transformers and lines strung across the dry fields like kite string wrapped on a ball, I would discover what I have lacked all my life, I would disappear willingly in the pure blaze. I know I would.

6.

The small exhaustions of the corn and soybeans should not fret me so. They have no interest in me, I have no power to help them. It's only this grim need to imagine the world as better than it is. A very loud crow demands most of my attention for a few moments, then a circling fly. Through the trees I see only a flat blue chunk of sky, giving up nothing of the stars behind it. Things die or persevere everywhere I know. Today, right now, I choose to sit in the shadow on the bank, but the dragonflies choose the sun and the river, and the fly chooses me.

7.

The latest theory, or so I hear, is that the oil and gas we claim to own are not prehistoric plants and animals cooked into black soup but leftovers of the earliest days of the earth, gathered in their pockets as the hot rock was cooling. There may be more than we ever dreamed. We may be able to keep the lights burning longer than we thought.

8.

The other latest theory is that the CO_2 piling up from all our burning is already changing everything, that we had better act fast if we don't want Saharas in Ohio and North Dakota, that we should leave the petroproducts in the ground and learn the "economy of fuel characteristic of uncivilized man." Try selling that to adolescent American males on Friday night.

9.

The farmers in Manitoba can look forward to planting early. Sooner than later we are able to change things we never dreamed. If we want to we can funnel Lake Michigan down the Mississippi to float barges or spray all of Texas from the air. Of course nothing is free. The doubters claim that the smoke of all our fires is circling and gathering like a great burning-glass, trying us in our own heat to see if we will take a temper.

10.

Say then that the gloomy ones are right about something, say the old weather we complained about so steadily turns out to be more and not less than we should have expected. Even so. We will not all die tomorrow. This could be the best and the last chance to change, as we have known we must change without accepting it for a long time. It could shake us out of our tedious and prodigal self-absorption, give us something to fight besides each other.

11.
Can we learn to love the earth with something approaching intelligence? Can we put the strength we have to work instead of blowing it up or burying it in silos like fatal treasure? Can we begin to trace the shining single net of things with fingers tender and alert enough to pull no thread loose to dangle, to walk light enough that the grasses lift themselves still whole behind our feet? Ah, we can.

12.
We have no choice but to think we can. It is not the war we expected. But it is the war the world has been trying to teach us to fight for thousands of years, and we are the enemy and the footsoldiers and the generals, and to win we must defeat ourselves first. We can learn to burn less, to burn clean, we can learn that when the smoke rises it does not just go away, we can learn the words it carries and make them say what we mean.

II

Inquiries into the Technology of Hell and Certain Rumors Recently Circulating

"The snowball arrives in hell every morning at 7."
    -Jack Spicer

And so they come up on us after we thought
we were free, better or not, after we thought
we had almost settled things. And they say:
We don't expect sympathy. We don't expect
trust, faith, any of that, we know how long
we made our gestures and you yawned, as bored
and unpersuaded as we were ourselves, needing
a new sign. You won't believe it. But here
it is anyway, the truth being a wall sometimes
for comfort and regret, some sort of answer.

It happened in hell, they say. That place.
You don't have to believe. But that day
it happened that a little boy was up
and roaming the great halls. Despite
the old sermons they were dim and almost
cool those mornings, waiting for the bell
to bring the fires back, the monotonous,
earnest screams. And there it was, you know,
they said, don't ask us why or how, it was,
white and eerie in that world of red
and black, steaming just a little, ready.

The technology of hell was barely medieval,
let alone postmodern. Enormous clumsy pipes
and hoppers, dirty yellow flames, everything
clogged and filthy with centuries when security
had never been a problem. So there was the little

night burn in an alcove, not even fenced off.
So there was the ball in the child's hands,
dripping, so cold. Why not? He was still young,
somehow. He remembered the year after Kennedy
died, how three boys with a bucket found the flame
on the grave that was advertised as eternal.
Play is a wild teacher. Of course he panicked
when the flame hissed and died. No matter.
In hell the gas had no metaphors or mercaptans:
it slipped into low spots, trying to think,
to remember. Who could have thought.

And so the staff awoke cold and confused,
and so hours passed as they blundered
through the blueprints, and so some ordinary
devil lit the match.
                            And so.
A snowball, a child, a match, and now
we come to see you, holding all this
like sacks of stale groceries, inventing
the questions you ought to ask: *Is it true*
that the maps are useless? That all
the old rooms are ash and splinters?
What is it that the wild ones taste
in the dust that settles from the hot wind?

We look at the floor, think of the children,
harrumph. We hint that we gave at the office.
And so they say: Fine. Don't worry. We will be
in the good room, plotting our course, laying
our claims, sorting our stories. We do not
insist you take this one as true. We do not
require or forbid you to gather at the river,
or kneel in the evening, or dust your shelves.
When you want to hear, we will tell you again.

Inquiry on the Fire Sermon

We all are burning, says the Buddha.
Fire in the hole. Fire on the mountain.
Fire in the sky, twisting. Flame that
lives at ten times our speed, and at the other end
Frost, good icy soul he, realizing 'the slow
smokeless burning of decay.' Wherever we turn,
and where we do not turn, there the fire
hunts and consumes. For the desk is on fire,
and the electric fan is on fire, and the Volvo
station wagon is on fire, and the Safeway store
with its glass and brick and tile and its rows
and rows of lights is burning, burning,
and smoke rises to film our eyes
until the mountains to the north are a dream
we remember only while we are sleeping.
And we burn to go there, we burn
the meat to make it good, we smoke the meat
to keep it good. We hunt with sticks
and harden them with fire, we wait
along thin trails for the small ones
and the big ones and we take what we can.
And the pickup truck with the hogs in the back
is on fire, and the ramps and slats of the dock
are on fire, and the man with the hammer
has a fire in his belly, and the eyes of the hogs
as the hammer comes down are burning, burning,
red with the flame that we pour from the skillet
and drink as it sears our throats and we cry
and we shout, we burn and the world burns
with us, it is right, it is good to burn.

In Response to Inquiries on the Dialectics of Consumption

Don't let them frighten you. This diet
will keep you alive for years. It has
some of everything you need badly,
almost nothing that kills quickly,
and a great deal of many things needed
to delay your pilgrimage to the small cell
without headroom or windows.

There are options—for example, white rice
boiled in river mud, with a side order
of three dozen bustling colonies
of untidy, fecund microorganisms,
every one of them natural, organic, and
completely free of preservatives,
every one yearning wildly for a dark
and quiet bowel to call its own.

Or Lizzie Borden's rancid mutton.
It gave her strength, determination,
and a vast sense of purpose, although
without clear benefit to her community,
the gene pool, or the food chain.

Go to the restaurant downtown
any night of the week. Add up
the grey heads bobbing above the Formica,
circling the salad bar, counting
their shrimp. Is this a health crisis?
They eat white bread twice a day,
and Twinkies for dessert.

True, your son is plumping nicely
on mother's milk. But how long

can that last? Ask him to start the car,
balance the checkbook, take and defend
a position on aid to the contras.
Before long he will be like you,
in need of every complication
and unlikely resource he can find.

Most of it passes through anyway,
or gets adjusted into flesh, teeth,
hair. It's a tough and versatile machine
you inhabit. It can handle far worse
than a few bulky molecules, a few
metallic atoms wandering through
like bowling balls among the chickens.

Granted, they tend to lurk in livers
like hoodlums in the Seven-Eleven,
cruise the bloodstream like teenagers
in hopped-up Novas looking for a good drunk
and a cheap fight. But remember,
when you walked in the city,
how many people did not assault you.
Remember how many of your friends
are not yet dying of anything.

Those traces that keep you up nights
all seemed like good ideas at the time.
Stop your agonizing. Get to know them.
Learn their stories, their myths
of creation and apocalypse.
They have things to teach you
about the landscapes of plenty and need,
the rickety vehicles of good intentions,
the hurt to be done just moving
through our delicate terrains.

Inquiry into Good Rains in August, or the Weeds

The weeds have staked out the beanfields
like gangs in L.A.—ragweed, buttonweed,
cockleburr, taller than the corn across
the road. They turn our optimistic rows
into a tangle of foreign territories,
more hostile and violent than any prairie.
They don't say thank you. They are not
refined. They stretch and preen like bullies
on the beach, hard and confident, dreaming
with dry joy of the gleaner who will cut them
at the ankles, break them loose for good,
set their children free to claim the world.

Inquiry into Simply Responding in the Negative

When the boss crooks his finger.
When your wife says much too sweetly
Honey? Could you come here a minute?
When your kids want read to,
played with, fed, cleaned, entertained.
Just say it.

When they ask you for money.
When they poke the knife and tell you what.
When they take it anyway.
When the hospital wants your insurance card.
When they say Lay down here.
When they roll up your sleeves.
When they start to cut.

You'll never be sorry.   Believe me.
They aren't worth it.   They don't care
about your welfare or the progress
of your soul.   Just say it.   Think
about the hours you sat in the car,
the thanks you got.

It's your turn.
Throw the envelopes with the whining
big-eyed children on them in the trash.
Declare yourself an interior exile.
When your mother wonders what happened
just say no.
When the capacity of the Ford station wagon
is just barely exceeded by the seven lovely
nymphets all eager for you to take them home
and it's two hours to curfew just say it.

You'll wind up miserable
and filled with poisons anyway.

It will make you better.
It will improve your digestion and lower
your triglycerides. Are you an American
or what? Remember the great
and enduring values on which
your fathers stood like the black muck
of Illinois, the generations
of dead flora and fauna who made it rich,
who might have been you.
The rotted, dark bluestem brooks nothing
it does not give the time of day.
If it could it would tell
how long the time for saying yes will be.

Inquiry into the Existential Maneuvers of Avians, or Honkers

They complain constantly, even though
they know everybody loves them,
because they know everybody
loves them. The heron is silent
for the same reason. The crow
noises at the edge of my senses,
clear on what he thinks of love.

Write the word for *page*
in any dead language you know.
The word for a short cloud
on the second day of spring,
the weather just at freezing,
the sweat of my run chilling
under my arms, the dozen new geese
nestled snug and happy in water
that would kill me in minutes.
The word for a quick moment
swimming freely in pure beauty,
for water falling four feet
and striking concrete.

The honkers give me some room,
not too much. They seem subdued
while I'm near. A quarter mile gone
I hear them burst out madly,
as though the king is dead
or a movie star is pregnant.
How well they have learned
to talk as loud as they want
and give nothing at all away.

Inquiry into the Origins of Hatred

Try this, then. Try breaking up floor tile
with a hammer for two days solid, twelve or
fifteen blows to each nine-inch square. Crawl
across the huge floor and address the gray
thick tile one by one, hard and dry and
stubborn, crumbling into powder and tiny bits,
refusing to come clean. Hit them, hit them,
until labor and fatigue and shock force a dark
pillar of tile and steel and contact, contact,
one hard kiss after another, up through your
arm, up through your spine, up into the soft
nest of your brain. Hit them with cunning,
with spite, hit them as you would your child
or your lover on the day when the rest of your
life collapses, hit them until your inner eye
is filled with the hammer head coming down,
down, and the shards cracking and scattering
at last. Then shovel and sweep and clean until
the black floor lies naked and ready for its
new skin. And walk out into the gray
afternoon, the laden skies, the thick drop of
water that bursts through the mesh of your cap
like that first, tentative blow.

Chainsaw Inquiries

What do chainsaws love?

> Lumber, dust. Live wood pulled down
> by the dying. Sun on last year's leaves.

Do chainsaws share a hidden fear?

> Rocks. Nails. A few, older, fear
> their appetites, and that what they chew
> does not nourish them.

If chainsaws dream, of what?

> Of hands that never tire, tanks
> that never empty. Forests
> rising quick as grass. A heaven
> where silence never falls.

Do chainsaws share a secret grief?

> They cannot hold what they eat,
> cannot keep what they kill.
> They cannot feed themselves.

Inquiries into the Technology of Beauty

(after Apollinaire)

I am going to explode. I have been instructed.
I have read Apollinaire in the original
and the 1980 University of California translation.
I have heard 'the thunder of the guns accomplishing
the terrible love of nations' and have seen
the shells bursting like flowers, like breasts,
I have learned that we 'must still consider Beauty
the one thing on earth which is never evil.'
I will be beautiful when I explode.

*

Remember the hole in the medicine cabinet,
the one you've casually stuffed
with razor blades all these years? How often
have you remembered them down there in the dark,
nudging together, rusting, sharpening
their secret grudges? They are eager
to show how deep they still can cut.
Their silvery arcs will glimmer, gay
as light flung by the dawn's fountain.

*

I don't need to explode. Spinning from beauty
are a thousand subtle strands. I can make you think only
of the delicate petals of prepubescent girls
for the rest of your life. You will steer
all conversations toward them, scrawl endless
mutant sonnets and rondels in their praise.
Your mother will move to Nevada in disgust.

Your best friends will pool their reputations
to buy plastic explosive for your last birthday,
and be acquitted to general rejoicing.

*

I don't want to explode. Instead
I will make you love me, and be the lover
of your father's direst fears. I won't show up
when you have the candles out and
the *coq au vin* simmering. I will call
two days later, neither penitent nor afraid.
I will write intricate, exhausting poems
from the front, detailing my suffering
and my vision of your black hair, your breasts,
sustaining me through the fire flowers
of flashing sleet. You will find the same poems
in the dresser of the redhaired nurse.

*

How war has nourished the art of invisibility.
The bomblets may even now be in your lawn.
Cunningly crafted of unsniffable plastic,
they will leap waist high like startled rabbits,
letting you glimpse their gorgeous symmetry.
The pellets tunnel flesh like wasps
through deadfall pears. Think of your children
as they flop and scream, think what delicate lines
the beauty of uncertainty will etch
between your brows. Don't be sorry.

*

27

Think of the wonder of the white missiles
arguing gravity into consent. Think of the beauty
of their smooth arc, classical, serene.
Think of the elegant use of space,
the fine metals crafted to silken tolerances,
the chips solving thousands of problems
at once and all gracefully, all beautifully,
all for a love that will spend the world
like a great bouquet of lilies and roses
to bring 'the terrible love of nations'
to you, to you, to you.

III

Inquiry into Faces, Light, the Guilt of Metaphor

"Metaphor is never innocent."
                    -Derrida

"I have never yet met a man who was quite awake.
How could I have looked him in the face?"
                    -Thoreau

And so what is a face?

   The baby gapes and startles as I bend to him.
   His whole being squirms, flowers into the grins
   and coos and wrinkles we use to claim each other.

And what face do you see when your eyes are closed?

   At the pool I put my glasses back on
   as soon as I'm out of the water.
   With the bench half between us
   I can't see the face of the young girl flirting
   down by the lifeguard's chair,
   and she can't see me studying
   her brown thighs, her haunches
   in the high-cut, thin black nylon.
   It's almost bliss.

And what face can you not quite picture?

   When we visit Aunt Velda she persists
   in cooking the whole time; we see her
   only when she finally calls us to table,
   and even then the eye sliced from an olive
   and placed artfully on the salmon loaf

31

demands our attention. We discuss
recipes and ingredients, the wine,
the placemats . . . . No. All is metaphor,
all metaphor is guilty, I am guilty
of making her into a metaphor which
she resembles only vaguely.
As well make her a flicker,
turning away in the clear light
after the thunderstorm,
when the fields are new-dusted
with not quite enough rain to satisfy them,
when the sun finds a last entrance
and can do nothing but look.

And so what are you doing?

    I am not quarrelling. Speech
is a violence, a yoking, vision
twines and grasps like bindweed in
the young wheat. Light is a theft,
a pillage. We use what we have.
I hold the child's eyes and talk
the nonsense we have taught him to love
and he drinks it in like milk,
waving everything that will move
and making all the good sounds he knows,
finding wider and wider grins,
flashing his gums and tongue
until even his joy tires me out.

And so what would you do?

    I would gather and sort and shape
and make something. From faces
I have studied, terrorized, ignored,

from light falling casual and burning
as sun on the garden in July, from tomatoes
and bindweed groping for water
they can push on into their seeds,
from these and my guilty selves:
to make a child whose face will blind me.

Inquiry into the Nurturing and Elimination of Life Forms within Marginally Controlled Ecosystems on the Fifteenth Anniversary of My Wedding

The baby roaches are dying
in the cold wastes of the downstairs
bathtub, accompanied only by
the diaper pail. My son hooks one leg
over the edge to observe them,
and my older son insists they're not
roaches though he doesn't know what else.
I don't say anything but hang up
my toothbrush. The guppies have finally
started breeding, and a dozen tiny blobs
of possibility lurk at the top of the tank.
My wife has cut plants loose for them
to hide in, bought baby fish food
at $1.69 the jar. Still their lives
are nervous: their parents love them
to death, and they must be drab, alert
and very quick if they want to keep eating.
In my role as haphazard wielder
of the power of life and death
over all species seeking to inhabit
the household, I turn back on my way
out the door to whack at a centipede.
I grab a flier from the wastebasket,
try to strike gently to avoid a smear.
Got it, I say, See you at lunch. Heading
out the door I kiss everyone quickly
wherever I can reach, hair or ears mostly,
and happy anniversary, I say.

Further Inquiries into the Nearest of the Energies of the Universe

"And if I die in Tennessee,
Ship me back by C.O.D.
My sins, they have overtaken me."
                                    -Norman Blake

At Bear Creek Park some fragments
of the bush persist amid
the football fields
and the high-tension lines
that buzz with their own importance
as I plod along under them.
I am trying to study the elements,
learning of the sexiness of fire,
the rubbing of two sorts of wood,
the spark. For everything is burning,
even the clear little stream here
into which I will not step twice
or even once unless I stumble.

The preacher yesterday
was big on the will
and our ability consciously
to refuse notions not conducive
to the mental health and Christian
prosperity of the suburbs.
Choose two things a day,
he said, not to worry about.
Being profligate I am choosing
only two things a day to worry.
Today I forgot the drought,
acid rain, forest decline, the ozone hole,

nuclear proliferation and the escalating
deadliness of all our means of inflicting pain
at short, middle or long range,
and worried the psychosocial difficulties
of children whose T-ball teams
are insufficiently oriented toward success
and the burdens that a needs test
for Social Security would place
on the independently fortunate.

Tomorrow I will worry
articulation agreements between
cocurricular academies and
the decline in standards for
compensating victims of Medicare
fraud. And when I finish I will
haul out my old records and sit
in the dark with my scruffy neo-
traditionalist hippie picker friends,
howl and twang with them until dawn.
And if the fire comes down
I will sing it into nothing,
I will smile every atom in the world
into a new morning, I will rise
as clean and well-pressed as
the preacher's suit, ready
to worry no more forever.

Inquiry on Infections

Just because you're paranoid
doesn't mean the dwarves
aren't after you. Just because
you can't see the writhing wraiths
on the kitchen counter,
the squirming vermin on
the toilet seat, the billions
and billions in the macaroni salad
ravenous for a new home to pollute
and ravage, doesn't mean
they aren't there. You
won't know names or faces;
your doctor will shake his
head and his hands as he peels
his rubber gloves, modern
times, he will say, some of
these beasties even
Maxwell's silver hammer
won't dent. We still have
options and strategies,
don't despair, it may cost
an arm, some hair, one
or two organs, but we can fight
dirty if we need to. Try
these first. If your
wastes turn green and black
flush quickly. If your
fingernails fall off
come back. If you wake up
in a cold, bitter land
where the very sky cracks
and sizzles, where

dark-clad humanoids cuff
and force you in chains
across a waste of rock,
stay calm. Try counting
the good you have taken
for granted. Try
to go back to sleep.
Try to keep walking.

Inquiry on the Son of a Practical Man

He was quick but reliably erratic,
if he'd just crashed home through the catcher's
glove to score he was sure next to fumble
a pop fly or throw six feet over someone's head.
Why just this moment he tried
to flick an ant off his pants
and left a thick and ugly gray stain
all over. Never mind. You go
with what got you here, and
so he goes. Glimpsing at straws,
grouching at streets, galumphing the sink
until black shreds of miserable stinky stuff
lie everywhere and his hands smell for hours
and he dabs at the floor with a washrag
he hopes he'll remember not to use
on his face later. He tries the tap again
and by God, the water fades down the trap
like a cockroach escaping the light, fluid
and beautiful in its flight toward the center.
He lets it run, dreaming its passage through
the sewer tile, through the leaky small-town
system, into bright sun and stink
at the treatment plant. He loses himself
in the laws of this world, that what
weighs most will sink, that what is small
and light enough will rise.

Inquiry on the Analogical Perspective, Or Why on This Day The Poet Will Enter No Complaints

Because the new green growth starts close to the ground, pushing
        its way skyward like any damn fool bent on ex-
        ceeding his grasp,

Because the trunk next to me has spat out clusters of thorns in
        every size from sixteen-penny down, determined
        not to be climbed whatever the cost,

Because some vine has oozed and threaded its way up despite all
        that, intimating that the only real defense is to
        have nothing anyone or any thing could want,
        including a place in the sun.

Because of the drive that pushes roots to do their work in dark-
        ness, to give all they find away, to ask back just
        enough to go on working,

Because such nobility allows me the pleasure of waxing eloquent
        in praise of emotions I will never share.

Because the creek is wide, free, slow and muddy as any poet
        could dream of being, drifting along into what-
        ever its banks demand.

Because the tiny chickadee, white bands on head and belly and a
        black choker under his chin like an old-time
        Mennonite preacher, fluttered close enough for
        me to hear his wings throb with his travels,

Because he would not stay.

Inquiry into Lagniappe

A little extra. As when the simple farm folk
lapse into sudden and iambic eloquence,
as when the snow falls all day in mid-April
in shaggy warm flakes that vanish an inch
from the ground. As when just as I've
opened my fly and begun I hear
the unmistakeable rattling of people
on the swinging bridge. As when
I smell wild garlic, fruity and rich,
and know I will not take it with me.
As when at the end of a day-long meeting,
headachy and near nauseous with half-
hearted attempts to breathe life into what
from all signs is a gaunt and odorous corpse,
I escape into the new oxygen of the weeds,
and the bees leave me more
or less alone, and a great black ant
crawls along the side of my log,
and a robin slides up the stream,
easy and silent. And the heavy bumblebees
and the prisons of my day dissolve
into warm, deep soil and new growth
stretching out like gentle thunder,
and I loll and lounge, laughing
in the palace I have not earned.

Inquiry into Keeping Time

At the hour the Gestapo favored
for crashing irrevocably into
the lives of the mainly innocent
the baby wakes screaming, coughs whoopily,
refuses to be calmed or comforted.
In the morning he's fine.

The older kids are scavenging again.
They collect jars filled with white powders
from the neighbors' trash, mix them
into potions guaranteed to finish
the bad guys that lurk everywhere.
"We don't drink them," Nathan reassures us.

Meanwhile, school has begun,
and I try the names like keys
I am not sure will fit.
My days are chopped like steak
for the stir-fry.
Carpenter ants have invaded
the bigger of the two new elms,
and the refrigerator piddles on the floor
at random intervals
like an old woman who deserves
our shamed pity.

Juggling unsteadily through it all,
filling my wastebasket with
dead opportunities, I tell myself
I can't complain. I have a new
big old desk, my computer still beeps
and shows green, most of my hopes

are still in the mail.
And once this summer
the band campers quit playing
and just counted, shouting all
together, the director shouting
over them all. When the horns
and drums burst back
into their heavy, obnoxious racket
I still heard the numbers,
the silent river running
below the music, secretly
keeping the time.

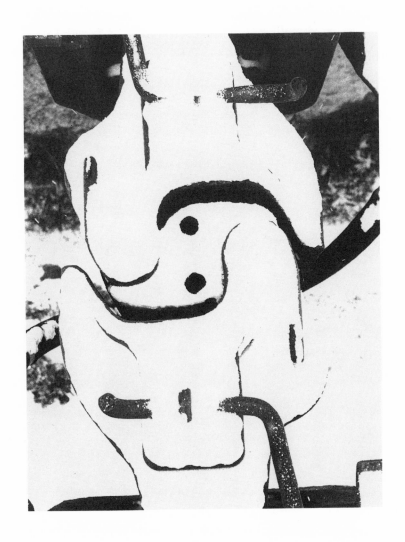

IV

Inquiry into the Discovery of the City into Which the Saints Have Been Said to Go, Marching

"Heaven is dead."
-Mallarmé

Don't ask how we did it. Call it fate or harmony
or tax dollars at work, the grasping that exceeds
our reach. Partly instrumental, partly mystic,
but we found it. And three days from the border,
on a wide, deserted, unworn road, the city.
The old black book had it right: fifteen hundred miles
on a side, the walls of seamless, dark green quartz,
the twelve pearl gates, the graceful buildings.
All that had changed was that everyone was gone.

We wandered far into the realm, across all sorts
of terrain, and found no other sign. The roads
all lead to the city, but moving out turn oddly vague
and hard to follow. There were a few early moments
when our instruments seemed to pick up haunting, near-
familiar songs, when we felt ourselves among mysteries.
Like most mysteries, they refused to come clean.

The press has floated many schemes for the place,
but all of them founder on logistics and supply:
the distances are huge, travel hard in the dark
and full moons. And while the city is great and glorious,
it lacks sewers, plumbing, stairways, public transport.
Some buildings are hollow, windowless husks, others filled
with tangles of shelves and pillars. No hospitals,
single-family homes, kitchens, parking lots.

47

And yet despite all we say they keep coming,
some with nothing but their hands, others lugging
pack frames full of nylon and freeze-dried food.
Bright tents dot the hillsides, and campstoves
glow and hiss at all hours. The climate is mild,
of course, and trees near the river bear fruit.
A pale sort of fungus can be gathered and eaten
though it won't keep. Nothing can be cultivated.

Still, if the place has defeated our usual interests,
no one has given up or died. The tourists avoid
the planned attractions and refuse to leave
when their money is gone. They walk the streets
wearing robes they bring or make somehow, talk
endlessly about truth and God and beauty. They sit
in circles picking banjos and dulcimers, singing
old gospel songs. They act for all the world
as if they mean to stay forever.

Inquiry into Lightness

(after Italo Calvino)

"Who pulls me down?"

We'll ignore what we can't avoid, stay
up late and talk, buy the piano
this week and starve next.
We'll find Dorothy, make her give us
the slippers and her beauty and her
magical friends. We'll tell Clark
we know his secret but will keep it
if he shares his powers. We'll take
two skips and jump and find
the purchase in the air we always
expected, leap out across the streets,
above the traffic and the others
who listen and obey, across the fields
and pastures to the deep and knowing
forests and the mountains
swirling in their stone and
up them with no strain,
no stopping, timberline and past,
beyond the snowfields,
past the highest caves
to shine among the ice and wind,
tomorrow and a day.

Inquiry into Damp Metaphysics, or Wheat and Chaff

On the coast this cloud cover is like a quilt
from your grandmother, more beautiful and useful
than you realize for years. And this is
the cloudy poem I've been trying to write
for three years now, the poem I left at home
when we came back out to see my in-laws
in Vancouver, the poem for Bear Creek Park
where two dozen acres of old forest survive
between the playing fields, the swimming pool,
the vast and complex playgrounds, the thousands
of flourishing and neatly groomed flowers.

And I run a little for the exercise and minimal
space for sweaty personal reflection, and then
I sit on a bench as a fine drizzle starts,
and the patches of brown grass drink it in,
and as the children yell and the couples stroll
I hear an odd little sentence: *To do
justice and not violence we must learn
to sort wheat from chaff.* And the mist
falls and carries me with it--*The grass
that goes brown first knows something*--
and I could swear I see the quiet,
fine streaming of the world into another
and back into itself. *People are not
wheat, not chaff,* I hear, as the little creek
moves so gently toward the great Pacific:
*Where the water turns across the rocks--
there is the place to start.*

Inquiry on the Proposition that All Things Work Together for the Glory of the Father

-for J.E.D.

A cardinal lights in a tree
no more than ten feet away,
but flies off at once, grousing.
He lurks. I have been quiet
for ten minutes now, and the bees
return to pull at the tiny fall blossoms.

My old teacher
saw two mothers die,
was beaten and shipped around
like the garbage barge.
Shot for mercy
his dog crawled home
through the snow
with half a face.

In the cold and grumpy dawns
of my freshman year he would
drag us through "Oh What
a Beautiful Morning"
in his baroque tenor.
He waved us grandly around and into
Jane Eyre and *Heart of Darkness*,
astonished by everything,
scandalized by our blank,
sheepish yearning to be told.
He signed my class card
every term, and smiled
and said "Survive."

I smiled back, and buckled
more or less down, and did.
I still tell his stories.
I never make my students sing.
Each Christmas I hug my parents
and sleep in a house
where all my dreams are calm.

He quit for the restaurant business,
went bankrupt. I heard vague stories
only, until I heard he'd been back
to the old school to talk, until
a friend pressed a tape on me today.
I listened as he mourned his losses,
talked about the incarnation, finally
asked everyone to sing
"When Peace Like a River,"
his voice rising over all the rest
like honey, like the wine
of flowers gathered and pressed
out of pain and time and beauty
that we all might drink somehow,
that we all might live some way
in the grace of things unseen,
in the peace we cannot understand.

Inquiry into What One Can Do with a Rented Jackhammer

It is almost fun, aside from the noise
which is stereotypically thunderous
and my general irritation at having
to mess around at all with this
rooting up footings through doorways
laid wrong due to the slovenly,
arrogant and slapdash work habits
of these overpriced big-city trades
who refuse to accept any responsibility
but to come late, throw together something
vaguely resembling the blueprints,
and contribute to the velocity
of currency circulation in the province
by being paid the instant they're
almost done. But never mind,
never mind, after a month when the framers
cunningly avoided showing up at all
my father-in-law is glad for anything
that happens. And here in the basement
with the rented electric jackhammer between
my legs things are definitely happening,
I have as big, noisy and irresistible a weapon
as any irritable pacifist could want.
The concrete is stubborn, young and strong,
giving up only puffs of dust at first,
but like a stupid but persistent teacher
the jackhammer makes the smallest flaws
mean something. Chunks of fresh rubble
give up one by one, and what was firm
and smooth and wrong gets carried up
and dumped along the foundation. We challenge
each other politely for the chance to hammer,

and before we know it's done and ready
for tomorrow's labor and mistakes.
We look over and approve, box the hammer up,
and leave humming with temporary power.

Inquiry into Praises

> "God is in the details."
> -Flaubert

The quarry is down four feet from normal
but the water that's left still nestles
to the limestone like a trusting child.
The tiny spider could care less
about the greenhouse effect or his grammar.

Football players across the county
are studying films, trying to heal up,
and not thinking about it.

The leaves gone brown and yellow and down,
floating out the breezy afternoon,
have begun to suspect that it won't
get any better than this.

The sisters kiss when they meet
and mean it.

Sunlight skips from the water,
finding new ways of being every second.

Wishing someone understood
the pit bull snaps at his food.

Bread in the ovens
is dreaming of knives.

If my feet were just a little lighter
I could dance anywhere.

The cardinal pecks in the dirt,
bright as any magazine,
satisfied as God in the world.

Inquiry into the Nature of Beauty, or the Tale of the King of the Cats

A man went on a journey to a mud-plump creek,
a man went with a weight upon him
he had no excuse or explanation for,
a man went stiff and somber
through a brilliant June day
and insects buzzed him till his ears
were red from his own boxing
and he studied the layers of trees and shadows
the muddy creek held up for anybody
and he half guessed at the names of trees,
maple, elm, sycamore.
And he remembered the story
of the great red oak someone chopped
and abandoned, how it was found
the next day, leaves crisping,
no explanation or excuse. And he thought
of the tale of the house cat who overheard
the odd story, "Tell Dimble that Dumble
is dead!" and spoke once:
"Then I'm the King of the Cats!"
and was gone up the chimney.
Hints, stories slippery as neutrinos,
sliding into and through us, leaving
changes we strain to notice:
Go, go, go, said Eliot's bird.
We crave only reality, said Thoreau.
We live, said the man, in the craving
that will kill us. The hard trunks
and the supple branches and the leaves moved
together, using all the light they had.

In one bank's shadow, trees and sky
and clouds laid their colors down
full and gentle on water only a crawdad
could love. The man thought: I am sad
because I meant to write today, and now
I have. Because of the cats. Because
beauty is not truth, or justice, or love.
Because it is something to love.

Inquiry into Gifts, or the Indigo Bunting

After hearing on the radio news
of the beautiful indigo bunting,
of its luminous blue-green splendor
that is visible only with the sun
at your back, I see one that very night
standing calmly on the lawn of a dream.
It knows full well how strange and rare
it is, knows it may live its days out
before anyone sees. As though
the world was made not to be noticed,
as though God had some job for us
beside seeing, as though eyes were given
for making the right turns and keeping
the rows straight. This is romantic,
isn't it? What can I say.
Some dumb gritty pressure,
habit or ideology, is warping me
toward a cautionary space where the birds
are all robins and grackles, beautiful
not even to each other, noisy
and jealous of their turf,
sure that if there is a God
he has done nothing for them lately.
I hear a strange bird call and
look toward the sun and see
a dark shadow, a figure that shakes
itself off to a further branch
before it even hears me looking,
to remind me that what is given in dreams
should not be expected again.